This book belongs to

Color Test Page

Dear Customer

 thousand thanks for purchasing this book, hich motivated us to continue providing utstanding products. We really appreciate our choice.

Ve are a young publisher but we have big earts and a big vision. We do our best to ffer the highest quality books for you to njoy. If you enjoy this book, please take a w seconds to share your exciting experience n the Amazon product page. This helps us eep improving our products, and help otential buyers to make confident decisions. Ve wish you a meaningful experience with his book. Thank you, again.

incerely

Iodern Art Publications

Credits

Delia W
1-7-20

DRAGON DAUGHTER II

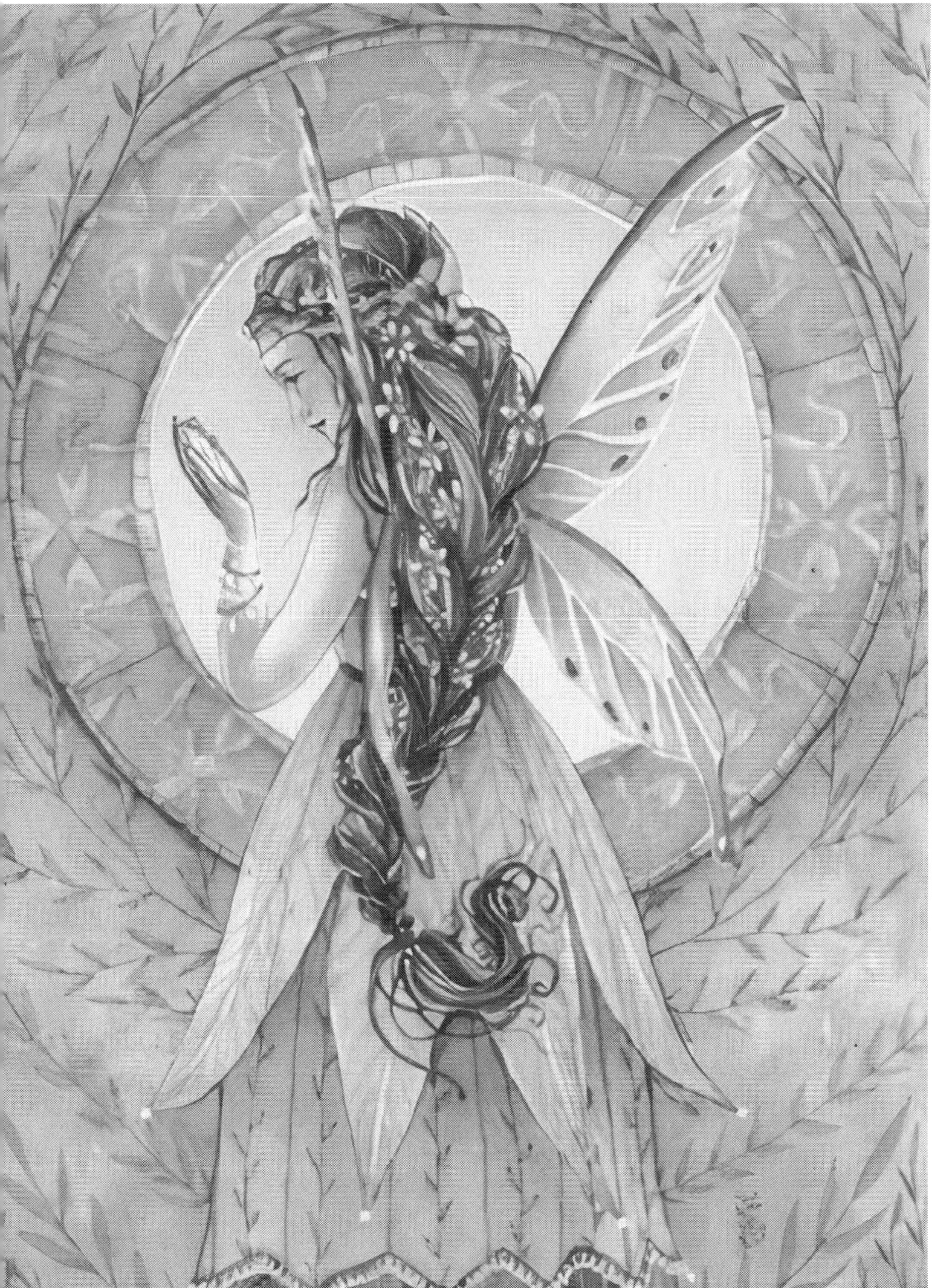

Made in the USA
Monee, IL
08 May 2022

96083747R00044